GW00686081

Test your

Emotional

Intelligence

JILL DANN

Series editors: GARETH LEWIS & GENE CROZIER

Hodder & Stoughton

A MEMBER OF THE HODDER HEADLINE GROUP

Orders: please contact Bookpoint Ltd, 130 Milton Park, Abingdon, Oxon OX14 4SB.
Telephone: (44) 01235 827720, Fax: (44) 01235 400454. Lines are open from 9.00 –6.00, Monday to Saturday, with a 24 hour message answering service.
Email address: orders@bookpoint.co.uk

British Library Cataloguing in Publication Data
A catalogue record for this title is available from The British Library

ISBN 0 340 802413

First published	2001
Impression number	10 9 8 7 6 5 4 3 2
Year	2004 2003 2002

Typeset by Fakenham Photosetting Limited, Fakenham, Norfolk.
Printed and bound in India by Replika Press Pvt Ltd., 100% EOU, Delhi-110 040 for Hodder & Stoughton Educational, a division of Hodder Headline plc, 338 Euston Road, London NW1 3BH.

Contents

Introduction

Why is Emotional Intelligence important?

Most people spend more time than they would like thinking about when they lost control or misunderstood others. To mature and to be congruent in the company of others, we each have to connect with our inner selves and our uniqueness.

A high Intelligence Quotient (IQ) is not enough to guarantee success in life. When you have a high Emotional Intelligence Quotient (EQ) you are adept at interpreting the emotional roots to your own thinking and behaviour and *choosing* your actions to influence outcomes. You are also capable of making good insights into the behaviour of others.

We all know that changing behaviour in a sustained and genuine way is extremely difficult. Change Agents need both a high EQ and practical techniques for dealing with others when stressed by change issues.

For many leading companies, EI has become the core of soft skills and management competencies. Whereas IQ is more or less a given, the good news is that EQ can be increased by your own development even as an adult. The distinction is about your way of *being*, not of *doing*.

Improvement cannot be achieved solely by attending a training course or reading a book to acquire knowledge. Skills associated with emotional intelligence develop throughout life. Training and sustained development activity at work can improve emotional competence. This makes assessments a valuable tool for identifying an individual's improvements and for measuring the effectiveness of organisational development programmes as a whole.

There is no single view of what EI is; there are a number of different views (as with many management topics). This book:

- Explains a number of the models, theories, assessment instruments and scoring systems. Providers place much emphasis on measurement of EQ. Assessments provide individual information through either self-scoring questionnaires or by 360° feedback (reverse appraisal of managers and feedback from peers as well as senior staff).
- Relates accounts of EI assessments from both individuals undertaking them or from practitioners utilising them during EI learning activities. Each account tells you what they did with the results, positive or negative plus their reaction to EI development activities. By focusing on *development* of EI, I believe that individuals, teams and organisations can reap transformational change.
- Allows you to complete 'EI Quizzes' with two parts of my five Genesis EI assessments. I have developed these from an EI programme designed by my Genesis team and I. (See *Understanding Emotional Intelligence in a Week* for more detail). This should assist you in answering the questions what are the benefits of assessing and developing your EQ and what are the pitfalls of not doing so?

Finally, I give advice to stimulate your thinking on what to do next.

Who should be reading this book?

1 All individuals committed to maximising their effectiveness as well as that of their staff.
2 All practitioners who seek to raise in others their self-awareness, self-control, social skills and intrapersonal capabilities.

Those who have no prior experience of assessments should read other titles from the Institute of Management series:

1 *Understanding Psychometric Testing in a Week,*
2 *Test Your Aptitude and Ability* and
3 *Test Your Potential.*

How should I use this book?

As you go through the book, ask yourself and make notes as they occur to you:

1 Do I want to know what my EQ is at present?

2 Does one of the different approaches to EI competency and assessment appeal to me through my values, beliefs and attitudes or through very tangible things such as alignment with my company's competency framework?

3 Do I want to develop my EQ as part of other development priorities such as professional skills

and knowledge? As you read, start to build a picture of the pay-off for you personally. Build your own Business Case by highlighting situations in your life that you could alleviate by managing them in a more emotionally intelligent way. This will help you to complete your next steps in the final chapter.

All enthusiasts, including me, will continue to redefine EI and to develop our models. If the choices in the next section seem confusing, don't panic. You wouldn't be happy with one choice of new car, vacation or food selection. So, shop around before you buy.

The different Emotional Intelligence Assessments

What are the different assessments for EQ?

The main EI schools of thought covered in this next section are:

- The BarOn Emotional Quotient Inventory (**EQ-i™**) – Dr Reuven Bar-On and Dr Steven Stein.
- The Emotional Competence Inventory (**ECI**) – Boyatzis, Goleman and Hay/McBer.
- The **EQ Map™** – Advanced Intelligence Technologies & Essi Systems, Orioli, Sawaf, and Cooper.
- The Emotional Intelligence Questionnaire (**EIQ™**) – Dulewicz and Higgs through ASE.
- The Multifactor Emotional Intelligence Scale (**MEIS™**) and the Mayer, Salovey and Caruso EI Test (**MSCEIT™**).

Illustrative examples of the different assessments are explained, along with their roots, models or competency frameworks. All of the above assessments, related feedback sessions and in-company EI development are available through accredited associates of the Institute of Management. An independently developed two-part EI quiz is provided for completion in Chapter 3 to give you an idea of the merit of assessment.

The EQ-i™

The personalities – Dr Reuven Bar-On, Dr Steven Stein and Multi-Health Systems Inc

Dr Reuven Bar-On is a clinical psychologist who, since 1980, has researched in more than 12 countries to develop a cross-cultural approach to describing and assessing the emotional, personal and social components of intelligent behaviour.

He started his enquiry looking into why some people have greater emotional wellbeing and greater success. He was equally interested as to why some with proven superior intellectual abilities seemed to fail in life. He coined the term 'EQ' ('Emotional Quotient') in 1985 to describe his approach to assessing this aspect of general intelligence:

'Emotional Intelligence reflects one's ability to deal with daily environment challenges and helps predict one's success in life, including professional and personal pursuits.'

Major factors of the Reuven Bar-On EI Model (measured by the BarOn EQ-i™)

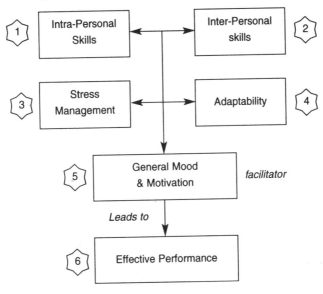

Dr Reuven Bar-On developed the Bar On EQ-i™ based on a comprehensive model of emotional and social intelligence (see graphic above and below). Reuven proposes that if an individual develops his or her EI competencies following the flow from 1 to 6 in the diagram above, then he or she will be more successful in life than an equivalent person of the same IQ. The composite scales are:

Reuven Bar-On EI Model (measured by the BarOn EQ-i™)

Intrapersonal	Interpersonal
• Self-regard	• Empathy
• Emotional self-awareness	• Social responsibility
	• Interpersonal relationship

• Assertiveness
• Independence
  (facilitator)
• Self-actualisation
  (facilitator)	

Stress Management • Stress tolerance • Impulse control	Adaptability • Reality testing • Flexibility • Problem solving

Like the EQ Map™ which we discuss later, Reuven recognises the strong relationship between stress management and EI.

The BarOn EQ-i™ is published through a Canadian company called Multi-Health Systems Inc (MHS). The MHS founder president is Dr Steven Stein, a clinical psychologist. He published a book in 2000 with Howard E Book, MD called *The EQ Edge* which chronicles the Bar-On competency model, scales and case studies. It applies the principles and practices of Rational Emotive Behaviour Therapy. It profiles different professions and illustrates how the information obtained is used to resolve chronic retention or other organisational problems. These profiles are drawn from a data pool of 42,000 people in 36 countries who have completed the BarOn EQ-i™ or its youth variant.

Studies
At a major Asian bank, a study compared emotional intelligence (EQ) and cognitive intelligence (IQ) as objective measures of work performance. It has scientifically

demonstrated that EQ is actually more important in predicting success in the workplace than IQ. Both Dr Stein and Dr Bar-On concluded that this latest finding additionally confirms the assessment's ability to predict success in various areas of life.

In an US Air Force study, EQ scores and actual recruitment quotas of Air Force recruiters were correlated. The EQ-i accounted for 45% of success in this worldwide study that included 1,171 Air Force recruiters. The best performing recruiters scored high on Assertiveness, Empathy, Interpersonal Relations, Problem Solving and Optimism.

In a third study, a group of engineers were tested with the BarOn EQ-i and given independent work evaluations. It had previously been thought that for technical jobs, such as engineering, these 'soft skills' or emotional intelligence skills were not relevant. This study found that the EQ-i could play a significant role in helping to select high performing engineers and to predict 'star performers' well in advance. The 'Adaptability' factor of the EQ-i was the best predictor of 'star performing' engineers, accounting for 25% of the variance.

With these three studies, it has been demonstrated that the ability of the EQ-i to predict job performance ranges from .47 to .56 (accounting for an average of 27% of the variance). Years of accumulated data on the ability of IQ to predict job performance ranges from only .20 to .30 (accounting for an average of only 6% of the variance).

For further reading on Reuven Bar-On, get *The Handbook of Emotional Intelligence: Theory, Development, Assessment, and Application at Home, School and in the Workplace* which is edited by Reuven Bar-On & James D A Parker. It is published by Jossey-Bass/Wiley (ISBN 0-7879-4984-1).

The scoring criteria
Generally, you will see that the ECI (covered next) concentrates on 'star performers' the higher your EI score across all competencies, the better are your chances of success in life. Bar-On challenges this and says that certain roles may benefit more from some low scores across a particular job profile. Bar-On quotes a debt collector as an example – too high a scoring on 'Empathy' as a competence may mean low returns from debtors. Debt-collecting firms will wish to hire and develop people with a specific profile suited to the work environment they will encounter.

The BarOn EQ-i™ consists of 133 items and takes approximately 30 minutes to complete. It renders an overall EQ score as well as scores for the following five composite scales and 15 subscales:

Intrapersonal Scales	*Interpersonal Scales*	*Adaptability Scales*
• Self-regard (subscale)	• Empathy	• Reality Testing
• Emotional Self Awareness	• Social Responsibility	• Flexibility
• Assertiveness	• Interpersonal Relationship	• Problem Solving
• Independence		
• Self-actualisation		

Stress Management Scales	General Mood Scales
• Stress Tolerance	• Optimism
• Impulse Control	• Happiness

These emotional intelligence scales are measured accurately with the aid of four validity indices and a sophisticated correction factor. Details of the assessments Internal Consistency, Test-retest Reliability, Concurrent Validity, Convergent and Divergent Validity are available from MHS, the provider.

How can the BarOn EQ-i™ be used?
The providers of this assessment suggest that:

- It can be employed in many ways and in a variety of settings, for example corporate, clinical, educational, medical and research settings.
- Potential users of the BarOn EQ-i™ include human resources professionals, organisational development consultants, career counsellors, guidance counsellors, psychologists, psychiatrists, physicians, and social workers. It is unclear if all these professional groups have used it to date.
- It can be used by organisations for screening as part of the recruiting process to aid in identifying potentially successful employees.
- It can identify those emotional and social skills that

are important to develop in employee training programmes, team building, and in enhancing managerial competencies at work.

- Research by Reuven Bar-On indicates that there is a strong correlation between emotional intelligence and job performance. You can create a profile of the top performers in your organisation to determine what skills are most valuable in your company or for any particular placement and succession planning.

I suggest that you check with your HR Department, at the time you want to use them, what the legality of use of these tools is for selection and recruitment. Chartered Occupational Psychologists have mixed opinions of any of these embryonic assessments.

Generally, individuals are differentiated in their EQ scores in the following areas: self-actualisation, optimism, self-regard, happiness and stress tolerance. Interestingly, they have not found any significant *racial* difference. We will look at cultural differences observed by practitioners in the next section.

Access choices
A number of accredited providers in the UK could organise access. This could be as part of a culture change project or routine employee and management development. You may choose to use MHS's Mail-In Scoring Service in which you purchase pre-paid scoring answer sheets. The BarOn EQ-i™ questionnaire is currently available in both Spanish and French versions.

The report of your choice is produced and returned to you via mail (expedited services are available):

1 Individual Summary Report
2 Development Report
3 Resource Report
4 Group Report.

Based on the volume of scoring you do, or if you need reports quickly, a computerised scoring programme for your PC is available. PeoplePro™ and PsychManager™ for Windows™ will administer, score and produce BarOn EQ-i™ reports minutes after a user has completed it.

The ECI

The personalities – Boyatzis, Goleman and Hay/McBer
Daniel Goleman, PhD, author of the business best-seller, *Emotional Intelligence – Why it can matter more than IQ* (1995) has also written *Working with Emotional Intelligence* (1998) which received a seismic scale response. For 12 years, Goleman covered the behavioural and brain sciences for *The New York Times*. Goleman also taught at Harvard where he received his doctorate under Hay/McBer's founder, David McClelland. More recently, Goleman has picked up McClelland's work on organisational climate and related it to EI competencies within leadership styles.

Professor Richard E Boyatzis's main areas of research are adult development and leadership. He is the author of numerous articles on human motivation, self-directed behaviour change, leadership, value trends, managerial competencies, power, alcohol and aggression, and a research book entitled, *The Competent Manager: A Model for Effective Performance*. He holds various senior posts at the Weatherhead School of Management at Case Western

Reserve University (CWRU). He was President and CEO of McBer & Co from 1976–87. From 1985–86, he was on the Board of the Hay Group when they were owned by Saatchi & Saatchi. Dave McClelland founded McBer which was acquired by Hay in 1985.

McClelland fathered the competency movement and triggered research on hundreds of thousands of workers in the last quarter of a century. In the UK, the term 'competences' is used in job descriptions by organisations to describe the outputs post-holders need to have. The term 'competencies' describe the input side of the same equation – fluid intelligence and associated behaviour, underlying capabilities and characteristics that enable us to deliver on the output competences.

In 1973, McClelland suggested looking at star performers. He initiated the concept of predicting how well people would perform on the job by using the competencies they display. In all the findings, a common core of personal and social abilities (Emotional Intelligence) has proven to be the essential ingredient in people's success.

Goleman defines EI thus:

> 'Emotional Intelligence is the capacity for recognising our own feelings and those of others, for motivating ourselves and for managing emotions well in ourselves and in our relationships.'

Boyatzis/Goleman consider an emotional competence to be a learned capability based on Emotional Intelligence that contributes to effective performance at work. Daniel Goleman and Hay/McBer have defined a set of emotional competencies which are the basis of the Emotional Competence Inventory (ECI) and differentiate individuals by his or her Emotional Intelligence. The framework falls into four clusters and each has a set of competencies:

Scoring criteria
To get the best use of the ECI, it is recommended that at least ten people, including yourself, complete an assessment on you. The Raters are made up of peers, family members, direct reports and bosses. This set of reverse appraisals is known as a 360° assessment. We discuss the pragmatics in the case study later in the book.

ECI Clusters
- **Self-awareness**: Capacity for understanding one's emotions, one's strengths, and one's weaknesses: Emotional Self-awareness, Accurate Self-assessment and Self-confidence.
- **Self-management**: Capacity for effectively managing one's motives and regulating one's behaviour: Self-control, Trustworthiness, Conscientiousness, Adaptability, Achievement Orientation and Initiative.
- **Social Awareness**: Capacity for understanding what others are saying and feeling and why they feel and act as they do – Empathy, Organisational Awareness and Service Orientation.
- **Social Skills**: Capacity for acting in such a way that one is able to get desired results from others and reach personal goals – Developing Others, Leadership, Influence, Communication, Change Catalyst, Conflict Management, Building Bonds and Teamwork and Collaboration.

Clusters 1 and 3 are about awareness of self and others. Clusters 2 and 4 are about management of self and others. Clusters 1 and 2 are about internal capabilities whilst 3 and 4 are externally manifested capabilities.

The competencies in the first three clusters must be in place in order for an individual to be effective in the last cluster. Goleman and Hay/McBer suggest that it is the competencies in the last cluster that drives organisational performance. Social skills are the competencies that leaders use to inspire people in organisations to greatness. It is the last cluster that successful salespeople use to build strong and profitable customer relationships. To achieve customer delight, employees need to deploy star performance in these skills every day.

Within each of the emotional competences there are 1–5 scales. The ECI gives you a description of the EI Competence Model, a Personal Summary, an in-depth review of the ratings for each cluster and a detail report on each item. A target level known as the Tipping Point is shown for each competence on the EI Competence Model page, the Personal Summary page and the Competency Detail pages. You do not need to have achieved the Tipping Point or above in every single one of the competencies in each cluster.

The report and your accredited coach guide you on the gaps, in order to find which competences are strongly advised for development and which others you should select in order to fulfil your role or ambitions. See later chapters for a case study to further your comprehension of this assessment. For example, you need all the competencies in the cluster 'Self-awareness' but only self-control plus two others of the six emotional competences in 'Self-management'

Statistics are provided on the number of invitations to complete an ECI on you that were distributed, received and processed. A familiarity assessment is also given which moderates the value you should place on the information and inferences made. For those reporting groups where more than one questionnaire was completed, an agreement bar chart is provided to show any diversity or correlation.

How can the ECI be used?
There are a number of accredited providers in the UK as Hay trains freelance consultants as well as their permanent staff. The service to you could be part of a culture change project or routine employee or management development programme. The ECI can be used to evaluate the individuals within an organisation, as well as the whole. Audits can provide an organisational profile for any size group within the company.

Coaches can use the ECI to provide precise and focused feedback on client's strengths and frailties. Based on your own comments and those of your manager, direct reports and peers, the ECI results indicate the specific learnable emotional competences to enhance your EI.

For organisations, internal (Hay-trained) and external consultants can use the ECI to diagnose an entire unit, profiling its overall strengths and development opportunities. Pooling the individual assessments of an entire work unit provides a comprehensive profile of the organisation's EI. This audit can reveal essential emotional gaps that may be limiting the performance effectiveness of the work force.

Much of Daniel Goleman's work is based on Hay/McBer's research. Most organisational competency models include a combination of knowledge-based competencies, cognitive ability and management skills. Emotional Intelligence competencies and the traditional competencies work together to give rounded capability.

To compete and to get ahead of the competition, the ECI and the model behind it can be used as part of an exercise in generating a view of what competencies your company needs for the future. A useful and popular exercise (from Hay/McBer and others) is to review your company competency model now. The examination would look at how and why Emotional Intelligence should either be considered critical or downplayed as appropriate. The cognitive competencies may actually be less important as differentiators of competitive edge and performance for a company than they previously were. Customers now expect more service even when purchasing products.

Case study
For example, one company asked me to design a Launch Event for a new management development programme. Goleman had been working with the executive level and had, I believe, influenced their company competency framework (see below) to include some of the ECI competencies in the four clusters described above.

Most of the 41 managers were at Level 4 in the company competence framework as described below. One or two of the managers were at Level 3 in one competence and others at 5. Our goal was to raise their self-awareness. We got them to look at the embedded and implied EI competence needed to achieve Level 4 in the company framework.

UK Company Competency Framework with EI competencies

Direction Setting
Level 4
- Explains strategic decisions meaningfully for others. Agrees business objectives and accountabilities with others. Involves others in business planning to gain commitment. Delegates appropriate workloads in line with individual accountabilities.

Developing Self and Others
Level 4
- Ensures opportunities for self and others to develop skills, confidence, performance and knowledge for the long term. Focuses own and others' efforts and learning on development issues which support evolving business strategy.

Communicating
Level 4
- Communicates effectively in a wide variety of situations. Displays confidence and conviction when presenting business cases and decisions. Communicates persuasively and with credibility when challenged. Maintains a network of colleagues inside the business and makes contacts externally.

Working With Others
Level 4

- Encourages co-operation between teams. Seeks opportunities to support other parts of the business. Broadens perspective to focus on common objectives. Is personally supportive of colleagues and strives to understand their needs and views. Confronts disagreements and conflict in an open and honest way.

Forward Thinking
Level 4

- Thinks outside of own business boundaries particularly when planning long-term. Considers a range of possible business situations and anticipates possible outcomes. Produces structured business plans and ensures resources are prepared in advance to implement plans.

Judgement
Level 4

- Questions and challenges others' decisions in an informed way. Probes and questions rigorously in order to get at the root of an issue. Analyses relationships between different parts of an issue.

Quality Focus
Level 4

- Agrees clear quality standards and reviews achievements against targets. Identifies obstacles to the implementation of quality solutions and helps to remove them. Encourages others to see quality as a means of gaining competitive advantage.

Achievement Orientation
Level 4
• Willingly takes on difficult challenges and accepts accountability for performance, sharing the credit with others. Projects realistic enthusiasm that encourages motivation in others.

Customer Orientation
Level 4
• Establishes business relationships with key internal and external customers, building and enhancing them over time. Ensures the message on the business benefits of superior customer service is constantly reinforced. Uses feedback to identify further service enhancements.

Change Orientation
Level 4
• Challenges current thinking and offers new alternatives. Helps new initiatives happen by translating concepts into practical steps and tangible outcomes that others can understand. Explores what is possible and delivers what needs to be done to make change a practical reality.

The EI competencies in the above model are at two levels: those overtly identified (such as Achievement Orientation described in the ECI) and those implied. For example,

Customer Orientation requires excellent relationship skills, empathy and resilience. The latter would be imperative if customer feedback is poor. The service team need to be led through re-engineering processes and revised customer-facing behaviours.

In this case study, we directed development of the 41 attendees at the Launch Event over the next three months back at work. This was achieved by enhancing the skills of the HR partners and the line managers. There was no further direct contact from us. We produced a bespoke workbook which included how to improve their own learning practice as well as a whole series of EI exercises. These were organised by their range of relationships: peers, direct reports (who were themselves managers), his or her line manager, family and friends.

This was independently evaluated and had pleasantly startling results for a relatively modest investment. Every one of the 41 interviewed reported improvements from transformational to specific benefits in self-awareness competencies and improved relationships.

Because of the company's budgetary constraints and limited access to the Internet, we chose to use a different assessment, the EQ Map™, which is self-scored and easy to administer (covered next). The facilitation of the event managed any potential misunderstandings about the differences in the models (Cooper and Sawaf versus Boyatzis and Goleman). Stretching them in this fashion gave them a deeper understanding of what EI means in their lives and behaviours regardless of different gurus' opinions or models.

Access choices
You may choose to use Hay's ECI pre-printed forms administered through your accredited coach or have your coach organise Web-based access with user ID and password security. The ECI questionnaire is also currently available in both Spanish and Portuguese versions.

The report of your choice is produced and returned to you via mail or handed to you by your coach:

1   Individual Feedback Reports
2   Work Force Audits.

The EQ Map™

The personalities – Orioli, Cooper and Sawaf
Esther Orioli, MS is a consultant, author, and founder of two successful international research and consulting firms. She is a recognised authority in leadership development, emotional intelligence, resiliency and stress.

In 1983, Orioli founded Essi Systems Inc. The company specialises in transforming workplace stress into optimal performance. Orioli promoted the revolutionary idea of positive stress performance and developed the StressMap®, the stress assessment instrument honoured with the National Health Information Award. The StressMap® has sold more than 400,000 copies.

Orioli's newest company, Q-Metrics LLC, was founded with Robert K Cooper, who is co-author of the book, *Executive EQ: Emotional Intelligence in Leadership and Organisations* with Sawaf. Orioli created the mapping technology at Essi Systems featured in the book and the EQ Map™ assessment. This is easy to administer, is self-scored and is a trademark of Advanced Intelligence Technologies (AIT) and Essi Systems Inc.

Dr Robert K Cooper is an advisor to organisational leaders, a public speaker and an independent scholar. He has spent more than two decades researching leadership, human systems, transformational learning and personal and interpersonal effectiveness under pressure. He is a co-founder, and Chair, of the Q-Metrics LLC Board.

Over the past decade, Dr Cooper has consulted for organisations worldwide. He has designed leadership development and professional education initiatives. In addition to *Executive EQ*, he is author of *The Performance Edge: New Strategies to Maximise Work Effectiveness and Competitive Advantage.*

Ayman Sawaf's personal story is inspiring. He is an international business leader who has started and run numerous successful enterprises in various sectors from entertainment to lighting. At the age of 35, Ayman realised that in spite of doing 'everything right' he was not living.

Fortunately, Ayman discovered emotional literacy and began a quest to learn everything he could about understanding, expressing and transforming emotions. Ayman found allies in leading authors and researchers and created The Foundation for Education in Emotional Literacy – FEEL. Since founding FEEL, Ayman has also 'mined' the concept of EQ and Emotional Literacy in print through co-authorship with Robert Cooper and authorship of the Enchante Emotional Literacy Series.

Exercises to increase Emotional Literacy and to understand

blanket emotions are covered in the Tuesday chapter of
Understanding Emotional Intelligence in a Week.

How can the EQ Map^TM be used?
Cooper says in *Executive EQ*, 'Business has become, during
the last century, the most powerful institution on the
planet.' The executive has to accept the full responsibility
that this brings in leading the way for society. The book
ends with Mahatma Gandhi's powerful quote 'You must *be*
the change you wish to see in the world.' This is an
important distinction – acquiring *knowledge* about EI
provides few benefits.

Cooper and Sawaf suggest that there are four cornerstones
to being a successful executive using your heart as well as
your head:

1 Emotional Literacy
2 Emotional Fitness
3 Emotional Depth
4 Emotional Alchemy.

You hire and judge people by their IQ, thinking that they
will turn around your business. However, failure in
forming team relationships stops any benefit. In this way it
has been shown that group EQ can actually be lower than
the sum of the individuals' EQ scores.

Researchers of EI have evidence that most intellectually
advanced individuals are often quite unsuccessful socially,
in both their business and private lives. Put simply, our
human lives are driven by the two forces: mind and soul,
intelligence and emotions. One of them is just not enough.

The EQ Map^TM can be used to advance Cooper's purpose:

the application of emotional intelligence in leadership, organisational learning and life. By being able to develop both the logical and emotional sides of your self, you can achieve a substantial breakthrough in the whole range of business and career development factors:

- Leadership
- Decision Making
- Open and Honest Communication
- Trusting Relationships and Teamwork
- Customer Loyalty
- Creativity and Innovation.

The scoring system
Cooper measures EQ using the EQ-Map™. Individuals score themselves against 20 scales of competence. The EQ-Map™ Interpretation Guide gives development advice on each scale to develop a 21-day action plan creating new 'good habits'.

EQ consists of five important dimensions:

- knowing one's emotions
- controlling ones emotions
- recognising emotions in others (empathy)
- controlling emotions in others
- self-motivation.

The results of completing the questionnaire are placed on the map scoring grid with four levels: Optimal, Proficient, Vulnerable or Caution. The score sheet can look like a map of the Himalayas. The 20 scales on the scoring grid are divided into five performance zones, with 2, 3 and 4 containing the EQ Map™ definition of the scope of Emotional Intelligence:

1 Current Environment, containing broader scales of Life Pressures and Life Satisfactions.
2 Awareness, containing EI scales of Emotional Self-awareness, Emotional Expression and Emotional Awareness of Others.
3 Competencies, containing EI scales of Intentionality, Creativity, Resilience, Interpersonal Connections and Constructive Discontent.
4 Values and Attitudes, containing EI scales of Outlook, Compassion, Intuition, Trust Radius, Personal Power, Integrated Self.
5 Outcomes, containing broader scales of General Health, Quality of Life, Relationship Quotient and Optimal Performance.

The assessment takes account of broader factors such as optimism or life pressures whilst planning development of EI. After a period of development of emotional competencies (3–10 months in my experience) corresponding changes appear in these broader factors. Showing its roots in the StressMap®, raising EQ through use of this assessment can reduce stress quite significantly. I have used it in my own company and with a number of clients. Further case studies and some experiences of professionals are described in later chapters.

Cooper encourages organisations to increase trust, to increase the capability of teams to work under pressure and to create the future through engendering initiative in people. He is strong on the business case for doing so.

Robert Cooper's EI Model: Three Driving Forces of Competitive Advantage (as measured by the EQ-Map™)

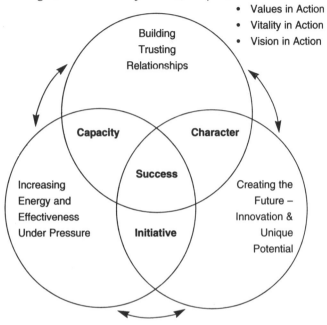

Cooper divides the 20 scales across his EI Model as follows:

- **Increasing energy and effectiveness under pressure**: The scale comprises broader measures of life pressure, life satisfactions, general health and optimal performance and emotional competence measures of emotional self-awareness, emotional expression and resilience.
- **Building trusting relationships**: The scale comprises emotional awareness of others, interpersonal connections, compassion, trust radius, integrated self and relationship quotient.

- **Creating the future (through innovation and capturing unique potential)**: The scale comprises intentionality, creativity, constructive discontent, outlook, intuition, personal power and quality of life.

An Interpretation Guide comes with each pack that directs people into development activities which help you toward the 'Three Driving Forces of Competitive Advantage'. See later chapters with real life accounts and guidance on extracting maximum value from use of this assessment.

The EIQ™

The personalities – Dulewicz and Higgs
Dr Malcolm Higgs is a Chartered Occupational Psychologist who has a background in Human Resource Management Practice. He is a member of Henley Management College's HR and Behaviour faculty in the UK.

Professor V Dulewicz is also a Chartered Occupational Psychologist and is Head of the HRM and Organisational Behaviour Faculty at Henley. Higgs and Dulewicz set out to examine the substance of EI, to resolve perceived contradictions and any ambiguities encountered concerning EI in the UK.

In Goleman's 'Working with Emotional Intelligence', a huge world-wide study of 286 organisations is reported where job competences of star performers at every level were analysed. Of the 20 or so common competences identified, all bar three were emotional competences. The most salient areas of Goleman's core competences are Self-awareness, Self-regulation, Self-motivation, Empathy and Social Skills.

Based on this, Higgs and Dulewicz define EI broadly in the following terms:

- knowing what you are feeling and being able to handle those feelings without having them overwhelm you
- being able to motivate yourself to get jobs done, be creative and perform at your peak
- sensing what others are feeling and handling relationships effectively.

Higgs and Dulewicz set out to correlate the success of UK executives using the data pool available at Henley. The results gave an initial confirmation of Goleman's core proposition that 'it is a combination of IQ and Emotional Intelligence which determines life success'.

As a result of research into predictors of success, Higgs and Dulewicz designed and developed a 70-item EQ questionnaire – the Emotional Intelligence Questionnaire (EIQ™). In their model of competencies illustrated overleaf and published in their book *Making Sense of Emotional Intelligence*, they set up distinctions of EQ, IQ and MQ (Management Intelligence). The authors give general development guidelines at the end of the book for the seven elements of Emotional Intelligence that they recognise.

ASE (part of Granada plc) market the EIQ™ Assessment and have launched a new 360° Emotional Intelligence General Product but details were not available at the time of writing.

IQ and MQ act as enablers with EQ in a pivotal position 'to pull together a wide range of aspects of the personality and skills of an individual in order to deliver superior performance'. Using the General Manager courses data pool, they tracked 100 managers from an original set of data in 1988 to their status and progress seven years later. Using a number of different measures of rate of advancement of these senior people, they found about 71% correlation with success across the three areas.

The Dulewicz and Higgs Model

Emotional Intelligence (EQ) – clusters	Intellectual Intelligence (IQ) – clusters	Management Intelligence (MQ) – clusters
• Self-awareness • Emotional Resilience • Motivation • Interpersonal Sensitivity • Influence • Decisiveness • Integrity • Leadership	• Analysis and Judgement • Planning and Organising • Risk-taking • Strategic Perspective	• Supervising • Communicating • Getting Results

Higgs and Dulewicz found sixteen emotional competencies that predicted success as a manager, which were shown to map onto six supra-competencies. When they looked at the overall predictors of success, they found that:

- 27% of the variance of success was predicted by IQ
- 16% was predicted by other management competencies
- 36% was predicted by the emotional competencies.

Furthermore, a combination of all three accounted for 71% of the variance. This is probably the maximum that can be explained when using this type of data. As predicted by Goleman, the most successful managers turned out to be those who combined a high level of emotional intelligence and an above average level of intellectual intelligence.

During 1998, the EIQ™ was piloted on 200 experienced managers on Henley Management College's MBA and executive programmes. Analysis of the data showed reliability coefficients within acceptable levels and construct validity was looked at using various personality measures. Overall there appeared to be wide ranging support for the constructs.

Predictive validity data showed that the EQ measure correlated highly significantly (0.49) with the overall EQ competencies identified in the author's original study. This provided a direct link from the questionnaire to the background research.

The scoring system of the Emotional Intelligence Questionnaire (EIQ™)
The EIQ™ has seven elements on which the respondent obtains a sten score. These seven elements are:

- **Self-awareness** – of own feelings and ability to control them. Includes a degree of self belief in one's own ability to manage emotions and to control one's impact in a work environment.

- **Emotional resilience** – the ability to perform consistently in a range of situations under pressure and to appropriately adapt behaviour. Includes ability to retain focus in the face of personal criticism.
- **Motivation** – drive and energy to achieve results, to make an impact and to balance short and long term goals.
- **Interpersonal Sensitivity** – to pay respect to others' needs and perceptions when arriving at decisions.
- **Influence** – the ability to persuade others to change a viewpoint where necessary.
- **Decisiveness** – the ability to arrive at clear decisions and to drive their implementation when presented with incomplete or ambiguous information, using both logic and emotion.
- **Conscientiousness and Integrity** – the ability to display clear commitment to a course of action in the face of challenge and to match words to deeds.

The results of each question are entered into the system from which a narrative report emerges and which gives instructions for interpretation and feedback to individuals and suggestions for development. The EIQ™ report provides:

- Details of performance on the seven element scales and an overall EIQ™ score
- information on how to interpret your overall score

from the data pool is given as well as developmental advice in each scale
• general development guidelines (what to do next)
• an Emotional Intelligence Report Profile Chart.

How can the EIQ™ be used?
Many of the current EI assessments do not have large UK databases (they are being built). The area of Emotional Intelligence is still a relatively new one in the UK but the ASE UK database has been built over a number of years. Currently, there is much research taking place both in the UK and abroad. Higgs and Dulewicz with ASE are committed to continuing their EI research and extending the data available to all those interested in this field. Henley's catchment group is comprised of international managers and contributors are welcome to add their data to the general data pool. Alternatively, a specific norm or a comparison group can be produced by ASE.

It is recommended that the individual use the EIQ™ report and that an ASE-accredited coach runs a feedback session as part of a much wider developmental process. Plenty of time must be allowed. Used correctly, the measure can provide some powerful insights into how an individual performs. The individual can produce constructive and useful development plans to begin integration, identifying which areas need further development and which areas of strength could be further built upon.

The MEIS and MSCEIT

The personalities – Mayer, Salovey and Caruso

Dr John D (Jack) Mayer and Peter Salovey put forward a theory that there are types of intelligence other than IQ, which was published in a series of scientific literature in 1990. They have developed assessment tools called the Multifactor Emotional Intelligence Scale (MEIS) and the Mayer, Salovey and Caruso's EI Test (MSCEIT).

David R Caruso of Work-Life Strategies has worked with them on the development of the latter assessment. The publisher of the MEIS is a human resources consulting firm known as Charles J Wolfe Associates, LLC.

They believe that EI is an intelligence that can be reliably and objectively measured, that emotions can help our cognition and that thinking can help our emotions. Mayer and Salovey have developed a broad framework of Emotional Intelligence that organises this work.

Dr Mayer views EI as:

'A psychological capacity for making sense of and using emotional information. As individuals we will all have different innate capacities for doing this and we can learn from life how to improve it through effort, practice and experience.'

An earlier scientific definition of EI comes from Martinez in 1977:

'... an array of non-cognitive skills, capabilities and competencies that influence a person's ability to cope with environmental demands and pressures.'

Scientists were trying to create a framework or logical grouping for capabilities other than IQ. Mayer, Salovey and Caruso distinguish themselves from the other EI thinkers listed here who focus on social *skills*, or outcomes such as improved teambuilding or personality traits such as optimism and outlook.

In a Chicago EI Conference paper in September 1999, Caruso wrote:

'... Heart and Head Combined

It is very important to understand that EI is not the opposite of intelligence, it is not the triumph of head over heart – it is the unique intersection of both. Emotional Intelligence combines emotion with intelligence ...

In this view, emotion and thinking work together: emotion assists thinking, and thinking can be used to analyse emotion. EI then is the ability to use your emotions to help solve problems and live a more effective life ...

... Emotions are nagging thoughts. Emotions are very often unwelcome guests in our lives. Yet, emotions provide us with information, which if ignored, can cause serious problems. If we are aware of our emotions, if we act on our emotions in a rational way, then we will increase the odds in our favour ...'

Professor Salovey's programme of research conducted in his laboratory concerns two general issues:

- the psychological significance and function of human moods and emotions and
- the application of principles derived from research in social/personality psychology to the promotion of health protective behaviours.

Salovey's recent work on emotion has focused on the ways in which feelings facilitate adaptive, cognitive and behavioural functioning. Professor Salovey's recent books include *Emotional Development and Emotional Intelligence: Educational Implications* (with David Sluyter), *The Psychology of Jealousy and Envy*, *The Remembered Self: Emotions and Memory in Personality* (with Jefferson A Singer).

The Multifactor EI Scale (MEIS^{TM}) scoring system
The MEIS is an ability test of EI and yields important information about skills which (prior to this instrument) were not defined or measured. The MEIS tests emotional literacy or emotional knowledge in a way I have not encountered in other EI assessments. In this sense, the MEIS feels similar to an IQ test but about different subjects. The tests cover perception of emotions, emotional knowledge and emotional literacy of complex and blanket emotions. It is unique in that respect and this makes it a useful *additional* test, say, with one of the 360° assessments. I found it immensely enjoyable and refreshing.

Multifactor Emotional Intelligence Scale

The MEIS™ consists of 12 sub-tests corresponding to branches of EI:
- identifying emotions in faces, music, designs and stories
- using emotions through synesthesia (a sensation produced in part of the body by stimulus elsewhere) and feeling biases
- understanding emotions such as complex blends, the progression of emotions into extremes, emotional transitions and perspectives on emotions
- managing emotions – managing your own emotions and managing the emotions of others.

The MEIS questionnaire
The MEIS questionnaire is split into five parts:

Part 1 – measures the ability to perceive accurately, appraise and express emotions' through what you see. The first part of the MEIS asks you to look at three different faces and to rate whether each of six emotions are definitely present or definitely not present on a five point rating scale. The best way to do this is to go with gut emotions and overcome any issues with picture quality.

Part 2 – also measures the 'ability to perceive accurately, appraise and express emotions' by reading through stories about people. You are asked to rate whether each of seven emotions is definitely or definitely not present on a five-point scale.

Part 3 – measures the 'ability to access and/or generate feelings when they facilitate thought'. You are asked to generate a range of emotions to a mild degree, not an extreme, and then to associate the feeling with words such as warm or cold, dark or light across the five-point scale. This is very interesting to experience but is nothing to be anxious about and may be quite difficult for some people. In this case, you are asked to answer as you *think* you would feel if you could *imagine the feeling*.

Part 4a – measures the 'ability to understand emotion and emotional knowledge'. Specifically, this part looks at complex emotions which are those emotions which, when explored, are actually made up of several distinct ones. For example, sadness most closely combines the emotions of disappointment and acceptance. Blanket emotions are those which we feel but get no useful insights from unless we are able to distinguish distinct emotions within them and discover what has triggered them, eg anger, frustration, jealousy, confusion. You may find it hard, but if you persist for a few seconds, you might distinguish the individual emotions which add up to the overall feeling. (I have included exercises to develop increased emotional literacy in *Understanding EI in a Week*.) Increased self-control, regulation and management are achieved through higher emotional literacy.

Part 4b – measures the 'ability to understand emotion and emotional knowledge' by measuring your ability to comprehend the progression of emotions from one state to an extreme. For example, happiness progresses from a sense of satisfaction, through contentment to joy and beyond into mania.

Part 5 – measures the 'ability to understand emotion and emotional knowledge' by measuring your ability to predict accurately the emotional states of others. You are asked to predict feelings that are *likely* rather than simply *possible* in a range of scenarios.

The MSCEIT™

In 1997, Mayer and Salovey posited a new theory that there are four branches of EI, in a hierarchical order from the least to most complex. Each of the branches in the diagram is viewed as an ability, not as a collection of personality traits:

'The ability to perceive emotions, to access and generate emotions to assist thought, to understand emotions and emotional knowledge, and to regulate emotions reflectively to promote emotional intellectual growth.'

The MEIS is being replaced by a second generation EI ability test still under development called the Mayer, Salovey and Caruso EI Test (MSCEIT™). The four-branch model illustrated in the diagram summarises EI as:

1 **Perceiving and Identifying Emotions** – the ability to recognise how you and those around you are feeling.
2 **Assimilating and Using Emotions** – the ability to generate emotion, and then reason with this emotion.
3 **Understanding Emotions** – the ability to understand complex emotions and emotional 'chains', how emotions transition from one stage to another.

4 Managing Emotions – the ability which allows you to manage emotions in yourself and in others.

The Mayer and Salovey Model: 'Other Intelligence' (1997)

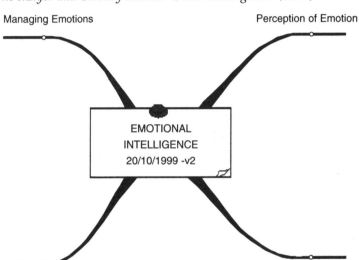

Managing Emotions

Perception of Emotion

EMOTIONAL
INTELLIGENCE
20/10/1999 -v2

Understanding Emotion

Integrating Emotion

Mayer has debated the conclusions of Goleman's EI work at Conferences in the USA and UK (with Goleman, Bar-On, Stein, Higgs and Dulewicz as part of the same discussion panel). The other EI models that we have covered so far have encompassed behaviours, skills, personality traits, outlook and outcomes. The authors of the MSCEIT see other experts as providing a mixed model approach rather than a pure model of another intelligence. (This may be based on the work of Davies, Stankov and Roberts in 1998 which casts doubt on the validity of mixed models.) Perhaps where they agree is that, using an ability-based approach or a broader framework, executive coaching or other guided development practices can successfully enhance emotional skills, emotional knowledge and EI competencies.

The MEIS/MSCEIT can be directly tied into development plans to expand emotional knowledge for leadership or team development, selection and career decisions. Acting on the results of the MEIS/MSCEIT, improvements have been reported in:

1 more effective team leadership and enhanced outcomes
2 reduction of aggressive acts
3 increased and broader socially supportive behaviour
4 enhanced empathy with customers and colleagues

I believe that the resulting MEIS or MSCEIT reports on your Emotional Intelligence skills and abilities would be a useful and complementary addition to any other assessments on leadership style, personality and learning styles or motivation.

The Genesis Assessments
Real life accounts of EI assessments

This next section will be helpful to you whether you are:

- a professional HR person investigating EI assessments for recruitment, selection, succession planning, leadership development, self-development or Personal Development Planning
- a business leader investigating how to change your company culture
- a junior manager interested in developing yourself more broadly and adding to your knowledge-based professional competencies or job-related skills.

To give you examples of what an intensive period of development is like, five accounts are related:

1 Two of the accounts of using EI assessments are clients taking part in a pilot for their respective companies (the Genesis programme designed by my consultancy company).

2 Two other accounts are from practitioners utilising EI assessments during learning activities. They are both very experienced organisational consultants; one with a clinical background, the other with a career spent with some of the biggest names in psychometric design.

3 Finally, I underscore usage of EI assessments with my own direct experience of running a culture change programme in my own company. This account goes on further to make distinctions in benefit experienced using both a self-scored assessment (the EQ Map™) and that of a 360° (ECI) assessment.

I have laid out the accounts as structured interviews with a list of questions followed by an answer. They cover what they did with the results of the EI assessment (both positive and negative) plus their reaction to directed EI development activity. By focussing on *development* of EI individuals, teams and organisations can reap transformational change.

360° instrument compared with self-scored
If you have decided that you want to use an assessment tool to check your current competency in EI and to review it periodically, then you have a choice between a 360° assessment or a self-scored only. If you are a line manager, the situation may be clear-cut. You can invite family members, peers, senior staff and reporting staff to complete a report on pre-printed paper or over the Internet. If you are self-employed, it is harder to get large samples because you work intensively on a project and do not get time to complete development activities. Often the team disperses quite quickly at the end. Feedback can be a short 2–4 hour session or part of an Executive Coaching or other programme.

If the gap analysis is significant between self-image and the combined opinion of others, a short feedback session is not advisable. If the results are shocking to the individual, they will effectively grieve for the former image they had of themselves. People go through a process of recycling the experience when they first learn of their fictitious image of themselves.

Examine the stages in the Kubler Ross Curve in the graphic overleaf. If you are the trainer or coach in these

The Kübler-Ross Change Curve

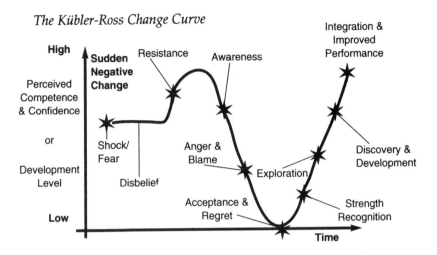

circumstances you need the skill to manage people through the curve. Each person will individually experience it in his or her own unique way, so the curve is simply a guide.

It is important that care is taken in the process of deconstructing the individual's behaviour, guiding him or her to insights and identifying emotional triggers from the past. (See *Understanding Emotional Intelligence in a Week*, Chapters Monday and Tuesday for further information.)

It should be borne in mind that most people do need a significant shift in their view of themselves to be capable of making significant beneficial changes. Emotional Intelligence is not the easiest option for such changes – alternative approaches are psychometric instruments and traditional management development learning activities. However, in my experience they do not enjoy such rapid and lasting success.

Account of Resources Manager in IT department, financial services sector

The following account concerns use of the self-scored EQ Map™ completed at the start and end (ten months into development) of the Genesis EI programme. The manager undertook eight (4 × 2 days) workshops over this period of time with 11 workbooks covering the subject matter and also directed exercises or assignments between courses.

His role had been badly matched to his personal style and preferences but he had soldiered on for a year. His company was undergoing major change both externally applied from the main group and from the market. His wife had recently had a second young child and they were both working very hard.

Question	Answer
Why did you do a management development course using an Emotional Intelligence approach?	*To further extend my knowledge of the individual and therefore organisational behaviour. To determine whether EQ could be used as a 'tangible' measure in terms of leadership development.*
What did your company believe they were going to get out of it?	*I believe the company at that particular time was interested in developing senior management with regards to their people skills. We also believed that EQ could fulfil that requirement.*
What was your reaction to the EQ Map when you first completed it?	*I found the EQ Map gave a dimension to my 'current state' in terms that I had not expressed before.*

Question	Answer
How did you find reading all the material associated with the map and the course prior to attending?	*The material was presented in a digestible format that made it easy to read.*
How did you find the language and terminology used in the map?	*Both the language and terminology were easy to understand – clarification of empathy being my only exception.*
What did you experience when you completed the map for the second time?	*I gained an appreciation of the value associated with focusing on a complementary attribute. I found myself surprised at the level of impact it had on a weaker one.*
Have you been able to manage your own development and are you consciously being more Emotionally Intelligent with people at work and at home?	*I am certainly more aware of my 'self' in terms of how I interact with colleagues, particularly when empathy is required.*
If you had the chance would you have preferred a 360° feedback version?	*On reflection, yes.*
How would you say you have changed?	*I tend to consider the recipient's perspective in any given situation; this has often resulted in a change of tack and sometimes even the desired outcome.*
What would others say about the change in you?	*Tolerance and improved communication skills (listening).*

Question	Answer
If you wanted more development in EI, what would it look like?	*I would like to have a programme specifically focused on how best to utilise EI to influence a desired change initiative within a given organisation.*
Would you prefer a mixed company setting next time or an in-company programme?	*I would always prefer a mixed setting. Members from the same organisations are likely to come with baggage or a hierarchical perspective. Both, I believe, diminish freedom of expression, essential if one is to determine one's current emotional positioning.*
Have you kept in touch with your buddy on development activities?	*Not as much as I would have liked. I feel this has been due to circumstance (we are both fathers) as opposed to real desire (and the speed at which my buddy has adopted modern communication channels getting on-line). This I feel sure will improve now things are becoming much more settled.*
Have you had any thoughts about spreading EI to others?	*Yes. I perceive the wider application as a complementary 'product' to help, say, a shift in organisational culture to a desired state. Example of a package: balanced scorecard (strategic/operational direction) as a competency-based performance management framework. EI is part of developing leadership skills required to manage the transition and understand the effects of change, empathy etc.*

Question	Answer
What advice would you give other middle managers considering developing themselves about use of EI assessments?	*Come with an open mind, leave your inhibitions behind, enjoy the experience and learn from within.*
Have you any other comments?	*I learnt a lot about myself during the course and have thought about the effects of the programme personally from time to time. Externally: the conclusion I have come to is that EI, packaged in isolation, could be difficult to absorb in terms of commercial value even though it clearly covers Self-awareness, Social Awareness, Self Management and Social Skills. The programme is an ideal addendum to an individual manager or leader who has consciously developed his or her leadership techniques.*

Account of Airline Executive

This client has a complex set of roles in his job. He is a retired fast-jet Military Pilot who now runs the operation of his airline at two national airports. He has quite significant man management and PR responsibilities as well as still flying three days a week. He is a father and his wife has started a new business. He undertook the same pilot programme as the previous manager (we have changed it based on their experience of it).

Question	Answer
Why did you do a management development course using an Emotional Intelligence approach?	*I wanted a fresh perspective on being a manager and thought that EI would be a different approach. I felt stale and wanted more information about myself as a manager. I was concerned that I was on a plateau.*
What did your company believe they were going to get out of it?	*The HR Director was running it as a pilot, if you'll excuse the pun. I wanted better man management in the company. The Training Pilot, my boss, also had organisational needs to be met.*
What was your reaction to the EQ Map when you first completed it?	*I found some items on my EQ Map were quite a surprise, but good insights and discoveries. As a pilot, I do lots of tests as part of Crew Resource Management. Because I train other pilots, it is important that I can look at how others are motivated and how they can work together as a cockpit team. Of the few airline accidents per year in the UK; many can be attributed to communication breakdowns in the cockpit (misunderstanding of content or preferences).*
How did you find reading all the material associated with the map and the course prior to attending?	*I found the fact that EI was learnable was fascinating. The airline world is focused on what makes people click as a team.*

Question	Answer
How did you find the language and terminology used in the map?	*The map language and terminology were relatively straightforward and interesting to see how they were grouped. A little bit of coaching aided interpretation. I found the interpretation relevant and plain English. However, I found the use of the word 'emotion' in Emotional Intelligence to be a bit pink and fluffy at first (not British chaps).*
What did you experience when you completed the map for the second time?	*I have increased my self-awareness and have become more self-probing. I have improved my leadership and management (being aware of my personal strengths and weaknesses).*
Have you been able to manage your own development and are you consciously being more Emotionally Intelligent with people at work and at home?	*The bit about deconstruction was most intriguing and I found it very useful. It was like choreography, pulling everything together. I look at the EQ Map and redress it each time, discussing progress.*
If you had the chance would you have preferred a 360° feedback version?	*Yes. Doing the course with people from outside the company was really good and allowed me to share experiences. It was most intimate and personal. In addition to this, the 360° feedback from within my professional and personal life would have been very useful (possibly painful but true).*

Question	Answer
How would you say you have changed?	*I have become more introspective and plan now how to deal with situations. It was a great revelation that it's OK to be angry (and I can express it, understand why and deal with it more maturely). I have changed in style. I am more involved with clearer guidelines for myself and in terms of experimentation. I am more self-searching as if I have been given more tools to work with. I take more risks with people management. I can be straight and assertive with people whereas before I may have 'iced over the muckheap'. I felt liberated after the course and more comfortable with myself.*
What would others say about the change in you?	*I have been told by a deputy of mine that I now ask for and act on feedback (appropriately). I am seen to be more reflective, learning and planning dialogue.*
If you wanted more development in EI, what would it look like?	*I would use the coaching skills in the programme to help others through the early stages. I would find this a bit scary but would prepare well and seek coaching for myself. I am very keen to get commitment from my top team to do the programme and then spread it through the company culture.*

Question	Answer
Would you prefer a mixed company setting next time or an in-company programme?	*There are pros and cons to both. It needs to be evaluated on a case by case basis and a choice would be nice. Doing the course with people from outside the company was really good and allowed me to share experiences. It was most intimate and personal. I found it very helpful discovering new ideas picked up on the programme. I kept it to the surface by asking for feedback.*
Have you kept in touch with your buddy on development activities?	*Not as much as I would like but comparing notes in completely different roles and industries is fascinating. I think we will always keep in touch and plan to get more organised.*
Have you had any thoughts about spreading EI to others?	*I would like to start with my teams at the two airports where I am Base Manager and as a Training Captain. EI is relevant to Crew Resource Management for the purposes of safer flying and teamwork in ground staff too.*
What advice would you give other middle managers considering developing themselves about use of EI assessments?	*Come with an open mind, leave your inhibitions behind, enjoy the experience and learn from within. To achieve a critical mass, you would need to select volunteers and make sure they are carefully filtered to get the ball rolling.*

Question	Answer
Have you any other comments?	The third phase of the EI programme needed to be longer as there was so much in it. We were feeling keen to get into topics in depth (Conflict Management, Stress Management, Influencing Skills, Negotiation, Assertiveness, etc). The facilitative style was very powerful on reflection but my comfort zone is with structure and being led. Pre-course reading material and fuller briefing would help set the context and prepare me for the course.

Experience of EI coaches using different assessment tools
The following accounts are from with one male and one female EI coach. They have run many development events in a wide range of industries and countries/cultures. They have used a range of EI assessments administered now to hundreds of people over two years (mainly the EQ Map™ and the BarOn EQ-i™).

With any of the assessment tools, the degree of self-awareness that exists at present in the person is key. The hardest aspect for coaches and trainers commencing EI development with people is to address low self-awareness. People's motivation to learn about themselves and become open to feedback has to be explored and any barriers to learning overcome. Without the right positioning of information on what will be experienced on an EI learning event in advance, individuals with low self-awareness sent by their organisation can be hugely disruptive. They will receive little personal benefit if they are not prepared to join in exercises designed to break the ice quickly and to generate insights to behaviour or personal discoveries.

Male practitioner
This coach has found that almost everybody who has used the EQ Map™ gained benefits as part of a programme. Coaching is essential. The results may prove mildly interesting doing the assessment as a self-development activity. However, it would be usual for the information to be quickly forgotten and not acted upon. In his opinion, the maximum benefit is as part of following and updating a Personal Development Plan (PDP) in a context with a coaching.

A coach's good facilitation and preparation can sort out any issues with the derivation of the map from stress management and the slightly emotive scales of 'Vulnerable' and 'Caution'.

The EQ Map™ (1996/7 Version 4.5) has been normalised on West Coast US and Canadian normative data. This can present a problem for Europeans especially non-English speaking ones. The language is Americanised and has a stylised use of words that can grate with some Europeans. Orioli's original research work investigated sources of stress and then developed an assessment tool for stress management. The technical manual demonstrates its roots in this research.

Stress is a perception and culturally sensitive so it is a tall order for this tool to meet the needs of global diversity. As the data pool grows through reported usage, the situation should improve. Thus, trainers will have to make less accommodation of these issues.

There is a degree of sophistication needed to bring self-scored instruments to life. It is not a task for a first-time coach. EI competencies need to be unravelled for people as the descriptions are sometimes abstract and not explained as fully as individuals might like in the Interpretation Guide. The subtlety and skill is in bringing real life examples to the mind of the individual, burning them into memory through experiential and emotional learning managed by the coach.

Inexperienced coaches who choose to do the three-day course to become qualified to run events using the EQ Map™ need to watch gaps in their change agency skills. Both coaches have come across trainers in difficult and unrewarding situations because they could not help attendees confront their change issues.

Usually, participants complete the map before the course and read the Interpretation Guide included in each EQ Map™ pack. The scoring of each EQ Map™ is processed and elicited through activities run by a facilitator in a development programme that is designed to result in a PDP. The provider does not process score sheets unless data is contributed.

The map (a single folded score sheet) gives a visual impression of how each item is connected to each other. If the quality and quantity of the facilitation is high the insights can be penetrating. (Having encountered this myself, I confirm this is so, see case study in Tuesday of *Understanding Emotional Intelligence in a Week*.)

Articles written by Richard Cooper and Ayman Sawaf make good pre-course reading (eg *Leadership Metrics – A Sampling of Data Points on the Value of Emotional Intelligence in Leadership and Organisations*). Investing in people can significantly pay back on the bottom line. Participants begin to understand the business case for such development using Cooper's model of the three circles and many case studies.

In summary of the self-scored assessment:

- It is a good relationship builder between the facilitator and the individual.
- It shows the relationship between EI competencies in a useful way for coaching.
- It is easy to administer.
- It is organic, flexible and systemic.
- The visual medium is very useful.
- It is a non-prescriptive part of the coaching process.
- It acts as a catalyst for some well-coached interventions – it opens up issues for review that may not have been thought of before.

360° assessments such as the BarOn EQ-i™ and the ECI produce personalised reports of some length. The deficits and positives are highlighted against quite wide normative databases.

They are well-researched and comprehensive instruments. The individual goes away with something tangible and sophisticated. Difficulties can arise with the quality of the feedback. Both coaches have observed that trainers are not always good at giving the feedback – they have seen people exposed and bruised; not supported enough. The assessments are robust and sophisticated so learning can be penetrating if enough care is given to the process of feedback.

The individual needs to be given time to understand the criteria and symbology of each instrument. Then the insights or observations from the scores need to be gleaned by skilful interventions. Follow-on exercises can be structured. They could evaluate which development priorities would be set to maximise performance in a chosen role.

This practitioner's personal style favours working with the EQ Map™ because of the importance he places on the coach/coachee relationship. Where the full reports are ordered, the 360° instruments give individuals more to work with *independently* of a training programme.

Female practitioner
When considering exploring and developing one's Emotional Intelligence, the reader needs to take into account:

1 the experience of using EI assessments in their industry, culture and roles
2 the [quality of] training of practitioners in use of these tools for assessment and development guidance
3 that it is possible to develop EI without having to use EI tests per se
4 EI culture change programmes can replace classic appraisal systems with a non-parental approach to 'slicing up the development cake' and performance management
5 the demographic trough in the 28–40 age range
6 the impact of cultural diversity and the use of EI in identifying, understanding and reconciling differences.

The bulk of companies are just beginning to catch on to the value in the employee lifecycle of EI competencies. I see many appraisal systems that take a parental approach which does not result in the development that people need. Use of EI assessments combined with learning events and coaching can produce more effective outcomes.

Much of the early work centred on stress indicators, employee well-being and pressure management indicators (Kerry Cooper and Steve Williams in the late 1980s). The roots of the EQ Map™ are in the Occupational Stress Indicator work. One interesting point is that employee well-being should be part of the Quality Model of the company. One client said that if you concentrated your effort on the quality of the experience at work and not on the outputs [as a manager] then you would achieve startling results.

Through a series of carefully managed interventions, an experienced coach can evaluate a person's EQ without use of an instrument. Exercises constructed of questions can elicit information about behaviour and its emotional or values-based roots. (For example, see the questions in Chapter 14 of *SQ – Spiritual Intelligence, The Ultimate Intelligence* by Danah Zohar and Ian Marshall, published by Bloomsbury.)

Classic appraisal systems and performance management can be replaced with a non-parental approach to 'slicing up the development cake' giving people the development that they need. In a culture of high EQ, individuals are very positively motivated to their own learning and proactive about it. The increase in e-learning spread through the Internet and company Intranets presents a host of opportunities in people's lives.

It will become increasingly important to attract and retain good staff. Great leadership practices are needed to get the extra mile out of each employee to deal with the shortage of 'gold collar' workers (ie MBAs) due to a demographic trough in the 28–40 age range. Most people know that they could give more intellectually and creatively (30% of effort and potential is not brought to work by most people). This missing potential is doubly grave when added to the demographic trough. Everyone will be in competition and chasing the same talent. Emotionally Intelligent policies aligned to values and a competency framework can give companies the edge they need.

An assessment which caters for the French, German and Ukraine cultures in Europe has not yet been produced by British and American providers. This normalisation is not to be confused with foreign language translations of, say, the EQ Map™ into French (ie for French Canadian) and Spanish (for American Spanish speakers).

1   For example, the life pressures questions are West Coast of America normalised. In comparison with the wine consumption of adults in West Coast America, consumption that would be considered modest drinking in France comes out as a Vulnerable or Caution score.

2   Another example is that the German culture is not an emotionally expressive one. This does not mean to say they are not self-aware or emotionally literate. It may be that they are not encouraged to speak out and openly describe their feelings in a work environment. They also may not do things consistently. The EQ Map™ gives you a scale of Optimal and Proficient, Vulnerable and Caution that do not account for this variability. During

development events, it would be important for the trainer/coach to link the results to organisational values as this sets the context for behaviour.

3 Relationships and extended family circles are very important in most European nations and this may not be accounted for in the present EI assessments. Leadership is also culturally-biased. For example, in France it is the norm to think in groups. Matters are debated and people have time to change their minds several times. They can air their views, absorb facts and nuances and reflect on the opinion of others. I perceive this as different to the more driven leadership styles of the USA and task orientation in the UK. There would be habitual differences in 'constructive discontent' and 'intentionality' due to differences in decision-making styles.

An astute trainer or designer would use EI competencies such as empathy and the emotional awareness of others to explore and unlock any cultural barriers. Even in its present cultural bias, the EQ Map™ can be used as a basis for dialogue. It can open a whole suite of topics on what kind of thinking and feeling behaviours create culture.

Used with other instruments such as Myers Briggs and lifestyle assessments, it can help people when they are entrenched. Coaches can use this information to link the strategy of the organisation to the individual (and their story). They can also map the thinking and feeling behaviours of the current and desired culture to the individual. This information can be used for development planning of the individual and, by further workshops, for organisational development purposes:

- EI assessments are very powerful in exploring issues of flexibility and trust. Lack of such values or limitations on trust radii can hold back large amounts of individual and team potential. Keeping an open mind is important for opportunity management and richer decisions.
- EI development can be used to redefine diversity – to encourage people to value differences and be more prepared to use empathy to gain true understanding. Can you understand yourself first? This is the test that EI demands as its starting basis.
- In merged organisations, enhancing EI is central to establishing relationships and building lasting bonds.

Increasing EI through development events is directly relevant to taking people through the process of understanding and reconciling multi-cultural differences. Comprehending how different socio-cultural groups have strengths that can be used to benefit the organisation, the group and the individual not only celebrates diversity but, I believe, evidences high EI. Not all EI techniques transfer from one part of the world to another and care must be taken in design to cater for this.

Where you are dealing with multiple nationalities and cultures, the work of Fons Trompenaars, (Intercultural Management Consulting) is very relevant. Transcultural competence equals the propensity to reconcile seemingly opposing values. This is very different to achieving a compromise.

In summary:

- True globalisation of a multi-national organisation takes specific know-how

- Be aware of cultural differences
- Respect those differences
- Reconcile cultural differences; do not accept compromise
- Test your propensity to generate an EI culture in your organisation as well your as proclivity to reconcile socio-cultural issues with your employees.

My personal experience
In this section I compare the benefits of a self-scored and of a 360° assessment for personal development.

Self-scored assessment
In the first months of a 12-month programme piloted in my own company, my own first experience of EI development was painful. The pain was caused by the shared learning curve of the two directors and four other people who worked with us regularly. We became aware of feelings, emotional self-expression and communication generally. However, the outcomes were completely changed teamwork and increased levels of trust. We were also more resilient under pressure in the following 18 months.

The self-scored EQ Map™ was used at the beginning and end of the Genesis EI development period. (The scope of the programme, having completed post-pilot redesign, is included in *Understanding Emotional Intelligence in a Week*, Thursday and Friday chapters.) The coach was experienced clinically in the National Health Service before moving to organisational consulting and EI.

Completed in advance of the first course, the emotive scale of the EQ Map™ and the cultural-bias did make me anxious. I had 'Life Pressures' and 'General Health' in Caution and four others in the 'Vulnerable' levels. It does feel very abstract to begin with. I was able to reflect on the 20 items in the Scoring Grid and think calmly of instances (events, repeated behaviour) when this competence evidenced itself. Despite the useful Interpretation Guide, it was through skilled facilitation that I was able to deconstruct puzzling 'bad habits'. I cannot imagine how an individual would achieve *lasting* benefit out of completing any self-scored assessment in isolation without facilitation and coaching. Pairing with someone really does help if they work with you or know you well.

Because we are systemic beings, if we improve what we are already good at, other factors also improve. The take that I put on selecting items to enhance is to use some of the items in Proficient and Optimal to increase those in lower levels. I did this several times throughout the programme generally taking two to three months to change my habits, mostly working in a co-coaching relationship in between the development events. Here is one example of how it worked for me.

By picking EQ Map™ competencies, I was able to create scenarios where they worked together and where I could achieve tangible results. Specifically:

- Interpersonal Connections is more than networking skills but includes how authentic you can be in these relationships, how intimate your dialogue is – risking emotional vulnerability for a network that sustains and supports you.
- Constructive Discontent means productive disagreement and the opposite of destructive content. It is valuable to disagree thoughtfully and

respectfully with team members to generate more robust solutions, to celebrate diversity of approach and experience.

- Personal Power is the degree to which you live the life you choose – do you set the direction of your life? Can you differentiate between things you can influence and those over which you can never have control?

Over an 11-month period, I raised these competencies from Proficient to Optimal by reflecting on present behaviour traits and how they could be different.

- **Interpersonal Connections:** I have always been a good networker. I possibly learned this when I lived abroad as a child and moved homes often as my father's RAF career took us to new places. I realised that I did not express necessarily thoughts and feelings with my fellow networkers or share any empathic thoughts I had about their situation. I realised that many women of my age have a support network through their children and that this was not open to me. I took the risk and reached out to three women in my life at the time – a peer, a 'client Boss' that year and someone who worked for me. The relationships began to grow or to deepen the moment I took the risk of sharing my feelings, insights and vulnerabilities. I still enjoy mutually rewarding, sustaining and completely honest relationships with them now. I realise now that because I kept a distance before or put on an act that I appeared not to need anyone, I was friendly but not so approachable. In the past and in my chosen career, I travel a lot and it would have hurt me to lose childhood relationships and to have had to start again. However, my adult relationships are more enduring. I work to create mutuality now and any inconveniences of geography, busy schedules or financial constraints melt away.

- **Constructive Discontent**: I learned to prepare more for meetings where there could be contentious issues on the agenda. I learned to suspend making a decision before I had truly listened and enquired into diverse opinions. My background is Irish and I have a Gaelic temperament that is quite passionate about many things. I reacted less to people's expression of strong emotion at work but still find this a development area. I ask more questions, summarise what I think I hear and am not offended if the summary leads people to reframe their point. I calm my gut reaction to opinions with which I disagree but I find this easier to do at work then in personal relationships.

- **Personal Power**: throughout the Genesis programme, I began to review my life. Was I doing what I really wanted to do? I had felt driven yet my full potential was not being recognised or utilised. I gave myself permission to experiment and to communicate my need to change things with people at work and in my personal life who were dependent on me. I was also coached to take compliments onboard and to not bounce back acknowledgement from others (it is like rejecting a beautiful gift). I also stopped trying to control things unnecessarily or to take on passive stress (being stressed by things over which I have no control nor truly affect me directly). I learned to let go more. I am still confronted by formal presentations and this is a development area for me. The development work is to envision myself mentally delivering a moving and powerful performance rather than conjure up an image of all the things that can go wrong.

I will continue to learn on all of the above but I can recall specific instances when 'being differently' about a situation served me better than doing something differently.

360° assessment
I chose the ECI assessment associated with Daniel Goleman's work for a 360° assessment. This focuses on benchmarking yourself against star performers. You can review the information made available by the ECI in a number of contexts:

1 A completely personal dimension in terms of your self-awareness, humanity and relationships with others.
2 A comparison of yourself with highly successful people generally.
3 Use of the ECI as a basis to construct a model of those emotional competencies that you see as vital to your chosen role. It would be wise to seek a coach experienced in the role or in development of people in it.
4 Alternatively, a different question can be explored. What are the competencies that make a difference to each of the roles that you currently undertake or may choose to pursue? What are the development implications for you to be a star performer in those roles? How much do you

want to be stretched? Which role will you pursue as a result?

5 For the purposes of organisational development, the ECI can be used to discover the Tipping Point in each organisation. The Tipping Point for each of the competencies is the point when behaviour is shifted from a previous state, when there is an observable difference and outcomes change in their culture. In other words, what it takes to be a star performer in each organisation is discovered. Clearly looking through the competencies again from a perspective of what is most important for specific roles is also valuable.

All of this individualises how to be a star performer in an organisation or generally in life. Based on the gap analysis, individuals can look at the gaps and makes decisions about how much they want to stretch themselves for roles.

Like many consultants, I have only once managed to get an Occupational Psychologist working on my team to collate opinions on me from the 40 managers, consultants and administrators. It was not feasible at that stage to use an instrument due to too many time pressures. Often the team disperses quite quickly. This year, I arranged to get an ECI completed with responses from two direct reports, two peers and a family member/business partner. Samples of ten or more are normally recommended.

The Personal Summary page of my report lists the clusters and each emotional competence in them. This is aligned to a level of performance rated by self and by the totality of others against a Tipping Point. The column marked Portfolio Components details what level of emotional competence you hold and what is needed. A tick box for the whole cluster indicates whether you have achieved all that you need in that cluster.

My results indicated that no further development was necessary in Self-Management and Social Skills to achieve star performer benchmark (Quadrants 2 and 4 in the Boyatzis/Goleman and Hay/McBer model). In the first quadrant, I was below the Tipping Point in Emotional Self-awareness, having two out of the required three self-awareness competences. Similarly, I had two out of the required three social-awareness competences and was below the Tipping Point in Empathy.

Whilst Quadrants 2 and 4 do not strictly need development, the competences below the Tipping Point might be pivotal for particular roles I play so they bear consideration. In my case, the Self-management ones were Conscientiousness, Adaptability and Initiative. The Social Skills ones were Conflict Management and Building Bonds. I consider these all very important for leadership roles that I undertake and for pure change management consultancy. I would therefore put them into my medium-term development plans.

My accredited coach made sure that I understood all the ECI nomenclature and terminology. During the feedback session on the ECI results, she asked me to think about the connection between all of the items which are below Tipping Point. For example: Emotional Self-expression, Empathy and Conflict Management.

- Telling people where I am emotionally by increased

self-expression will assist with conflict management. Disclosure of feelings is often very powerful in drawing out what concerns others. Empathy can often inform what is best to disclose in order to unlock particular situations. I can become more empathic and check out the emotional status of others.

- What are the triggers that cause misdirected anger? When I feel like this what does this do to me and the work I do?
- If I am making a judgement, do I need to explain my thinking and feelings to others more in the process?

I will go on to look at a sensitivity analysis of the most significant competencies for important roles. However, immediate development activity has arisen for short-term activity from my co-coaching relationship with another consultant. Having reviewed the ECI report together, my coach asked me to reflect on the following questions:

1 Which situational factors affect my stress levels?
2 When am I completely relaxed?
3 When am I out of control and completely irrational?
4 What are the physiological symptoms and what are the psychological? I am to record all of them so that I have a continuum from lucid to irrational and unregulated.

Having reviewed the ECI Comments Report that lists (by category of Rater) their perception of my strengths and weaknesses, I was to then become two people – participant and observer for seven to ten days.

5 In my own words, what would be the payoff for making the changes highlighted in the ECI?

6 What does it cost me when I revert to less emotionally intelligent behaviour? For example, the price could be all the self-negating behaviours.

I found this extremely useful as it made me realise a lot of things. It made me admit what I already knew and did not accommodate sufficiently well. I am quite claustrophobic. I sense fear, panic and aggression when feeling crowded or unable to direct my own path. Having come from an Armed Forces family background and having had a first career as a Naval Officer where security was high, part of me has found self-employment very challenging.

Because my behaviour can drop back under pressure, I also need to consider better time management to cater for the frequent and unexpected extra workloads that my business places on me. I think this would also allow me to relax with less guilt. My coach also recommended that my husband and I overtly practice more positive affirmation. I have begun this on a daily basis and whilst it feels strange, I swear that my brain chemistry feels happier already. We seem to be more affectionate and supportive together even when the pressure is really on.

I still have a lot of useful information to take from the ECI and I have found it very intriguing. I thoroughly enjoyed my in-company EI programme which used the EQ Map™ at that time. The skilled facilitation and 'buddying' helped me to extract the maximum learning from the visual medium of the score sheet. I would not have gained such wide-ranging benefits without the development activities both in workshops and directed post-course development.

A unique EQ test now follows which uses the competence

framework that I started in *Understanding Emotional Intelligence in a Week*. It is not meant to be as serious as the series of assessments described in the first section. However, you should be able to get a flavour for your current emotional capabilities. It is in two parts: Self-awareness and Self-control.

Developing your Emotional Intelligence Quiz

The first half of this quiz tests your self-awareness competencies: awareness of feelings, personal insight and self-assurance. Tick one response to each question, 1–20. Using the legend below, add up your score selecting the corresponding commentary as a guide to your present level and needs.

Grade	Legend and scoring instructions	Score
Always	There are no exceptions, you would have to think consciously about behaving any other way and changing what you have always done.	Add 4 points for every tick
Routinely	Every week you would present yourself this way or react this way with few exceptions.	Add 3 points for every tick
Sometimes	At your best, this is what you would be seen doing.	Add 2 points for every tick
Rarely	It would be considered unusual for this to be what you say, think or do.	Add 1 point for every tick
Never	There would be no exceptions; you do not present this way to people at any time.	No points

Awareness of feelings: Recognising one's emotions, their effects and capability to deal with them.

Self-awareness competencies	Never	Rarely	Some-times	Routinely	Always
1 Do you know which emotions you are feeling and can you accurately label them individually?	☐	☐	☐	☐	☐
2 Can you say why you are feeling those emotions?	☐	☐	☐	☐	☐
3 Do you recognise the chain from experiencing an emotion to taking action based on it (ie the links between your feelings and what you think, do, and say)?	☐	☐	☐	☐	☐
4 Do you recognise how your feelings affect your performance, the quality of experience at work and your relationships?	☐	☐	☐	☐	☐
5 Do you have a guiding awareness of your values or goals	☐	☐	☐	☐	☐
6 Are you aware of any gaps between espoused values & actual behaviour?	☐	☐	☐	☐	☐

Personal insight: Knowing one's key strengths and frailties.

Self-awareness competencies	Never	Rarely	Some-times	Routinely	Always
7 Are you aware of your strengths and weaknesses to the degree that others familiar with you would agree with you?	☐	☐	☐	☐	☐
8 To what extent do you make decisions in relationships based on your values? (ie experience emotional boundaries in relationships.)	☐	☐	☐	☐	☐
9 Are you, or do you consciously make time to be reflective? (Understanding the power of learning from experience even if reflection is not your natural style?)	☐	☐	☐	☐	☐
10 Are you open to candid feedback?	☐	☐	☐	☐	☐
11 Are you objective about others feedback and able to generate positive strokes for yourself appropriately?	☐	☐	☐	☐	☐

Self-awareness competencies	Never	Rarely	Some-times	Routinely	Always
12 Are you open to new perspectives?	☐	☐	☐	☐	☐
13 Are you committed to continuous learning and self-development?	☐	☐	☐	☐	☐
14 Would others say that you show a perspective about yourself and a sense of humour?	☐	☐	☐	☐	☐

Self-assurance: Sureness about one's self-worth and capabilities.

Self-awareness competencies	Never	Rarely	Some-times	Routinely	Always
15 Do you present yourself with self-possession; have poise but with warmth?	☐	☐	☐	☐	☐
16 Can you celebrate diversity in personal and professional life?	☐	☐	☐	☐	☐
17 Do you voice views that are unpopular and go out on a limb for what is right?	☐	☐	☐	☐	☐
18 Are you decisive using emotional and analytical information and able to make sound judgements?	☐	☐	☐	☐	☐

Self-awareness competencies	Never	Rarely	Some-times	Routinely	Always
19 Are you decisive despite uncertainties (perceptions of risk) and pressures?	☐	☐	☐	☐	☐
20 Are you generally recognised as self-confident?	☐	☐	☐	☐	☐

Self-awareness scores

Score = 80–60

Congratulations! You have a high to exceptional awareness of your own emotions, thoughts and resulting behaviour. You would have the ability to reflect on incidents that did not go well or did not go as expected and to analyse your part in that sequence of events. You would recognise the difference between *doing* something differently and *being* differently about something.

You would monitor your attitude and think about how it affected your performance and how it resulted in an unexpected response from others. You may only be self-aware after an event when you get flashes of inspiration about what you could have done differently.

Your developmental step is to become self-aware either prior to, or during, an unhelpful interaction. You will be able to use your increased self-awareness to gain improved self-regulation in managing your emotions and holding back unhelpful impulses. You probably prepare for potential conflict by thinking out what could happen and devising tactics or strategies to achieve more helpful outcomes.

Score = 59–40
Well done, you should be pleased with the results and these
would reflect the quality of your relationships at work,
home and socially. If you find that relationships are of
concern, then review your quiz responses when you have
some time set aside for yourself. You should as a rule
have answered most questions as 'routinely' or
'sometimes'.

Reflect on the reasons that you put a 'sometimes' response.
Write down specific incidents that remind you of times
when you did not display emotionally intelligent
behaviour. Think about the environment you were in and
write down what negative influences were acting on you.
Record both your physical and mental state. Think back to
incidents as a child that led you to have moments of
personal insight and self-discovery.

Think about the behaviour of others and record what
triggered emotions and unhelpful responses in you. If
possible, enrol others in helping you to relive an event in
slow motion for the purpose of greater understanding.
Think about questions that you could ask others in the
future to check out how you are coming across and being
understood.

In the future, try to stop yourself proactively from repeating
mistakes. Alternatively, catch yourself in the middle and
calm yourself or ask for co-operation in others to avoid a
poor outcome. Preparing and rehearsing for handling
difficult interactions may well be very rewarding. Do not be
shy to ask for help from those that you perceive as having
greater skill than your own.

Score = 39–20
The way you act or the responses that you get from others may puzzle you. You may feel misunderstood a significant amount of the time and not understand what you do that gets you the frequently occurring results. Enlist the help of a friend. Get them to complete the questionnaire as if they are scoring it about you. Go through the responses and discuss with them what happens to you by reflecting on specific events that you have shared or that have been reported by others.

Score = 19–0
Thank you for being so honest. Showing integrity is a great EI strength. You would benefit from doing the exercises in the *Understanding Emotional Intelligence in a Week* book for a period of three months. Alternatively or in addition, doing a course would help you to increase your self-awareness and prepare you to develop your EQ further at home and at work. This score does not mean that you necessarily have poor social skills in relating to others, just that you are not particularly aware of how or why you behave the way you do.

The second half covers self-control competencies: self-regulation, authenticity, accountability, flexibility and self-motivation. Tick a single response to each question 21–43. Using the legend, add up your score selecting the corresponding commentary, as a guide to your present self-control and development needs.

Self-regulation: Managing emotions and holding back unhelpful impulses.

Self-control competencies	Never	Rarely	Some-times	Routinely	Always
21 Are you able to stop acting on impulse?	☐	☐	☐	☐	☐
22 Are you able to remain collected, positive and unflustered even at testing times?	☐	☐	☐	☐	☐
23 Are you able to identify when your behaviour is unproductive or unhelpful?	☐	☐	☐	☐	☐
24 Do you manage distressing emotions well, reducing anxiety associated with these situations?	☐	☐	☐	☐	☐
25 Would others say that you are capable of remaining lucid and focused under pressure?	☐	☐	☐	☐	☐

Authenticity: Being true to yourself and others.

Self-control competencies	Never	Rarely	Some-times	Routinely	Always
26 Are you able to build trust by displaying congruent behaviour, ie by your words and actions being aligned?	☐	☐	☐	☐	☐

Self-control competencies	Never	Rarely	Some-times	Routinely	Always
27 Would others say you are beyond reproach, acting ethically and that you are challenging of your own motives?	☐	☐	☐	☐	☐
28 Even when in the minority, are you capable of standing up for your values?	☐	☐	☐	☐	☐
29 When you slip back to old bad habits, do you have a sense of humour and some compassion about it?	☐	☐	☐	☐	☐

Accountability: Taking responsibility, owning your performance.

Self-control competencies	Never	Rarely	Some-times	Routinely	Always
30 Do you take responsibility for your actions and inaction where appropriate?	☐	☐	☐	☐	☐
31 Do you clear up assumptions and misconceptions?	☐	☐	☐	☐	☐
32 Do you keep promises?	☐	☐	☐	☐	☐
33 Do you hold yourself accountable to objectives?	☐	☐	☐	☐	☐

Self-control competencies	Never	Rarely	Some-times	Routinely	Always
34 Would others say that you prioritise what is important or urgent (or both) every day?	☐	☐	☐	☐	☐

Flexibility: The ability to embrace and adapt to change including overcoming barriers.

Self-control competencies	Never	Rarely	Some-times	Routinely	Always
35 Do you allow for change in plans and accept the need for some uncertainty?	☐	☐	☐	☐	☐
36 Are you capable of letting go of hobby horses and accepting shifting priorities during a challenging period of change?	☐	☐	☐	☐	☐
37 Are you adaptable in how you perceive events or different peoples?	☐	☐	☐	☐	☐
38 Are you open to issues that confront you with personal implications?	☐	☐	☐	☐	☐
39 Do you explore your personal issues with others?	☐	☐	☐	☐	☐

Self-motivation: Positively managing your outlook.

Self-control competencies	Never	Rarely	Some-times	Routinely	Always
40 Are you driven to improve and meet high standards?	☐	☐	☐	☐	☐
41 Would people say that you look for the opportunity first before the problem?	☐	☐	☐	☐	☐
42 Do you demonstrate commitment in relationships and explore barriers and boundaries?	☐	☐	☐	☐	☐
43 Do you show persistence in overcoming setbacks and pursuing positive outcomes?	☐	☐	☐	☐	☐

Self-control scores

Score = 88–66

If you have answered most questions as Always or Routinely – congratulations! (If you have achieved this score through a wide variation of responses [noughts and fours] you should look at the development guidance in the other Score Guides as well.) You have a high to exceptional capability to moderate your behaviour. You would have the ability to reflect on incidents that did not go well and to analyse the chain of emotions which lead to unhelpful behaviour. You would recognise when the chain could have been broken and the point at which you could have chosen to behave differently.

If your ability for self-control is combined with a high self-awareness (and it is not necessarily so in all cases) then your developmental areas will be to increase your awareness of others and your social skills. You can also increase your coaching capability so that you can help others achieve what you have achieved for yourself.

Subjects for development: mentoring, being a role model, coaching skills, facilitation, change agency. Generate a development plan around those aspects of any competence that you have had lower scores in which includes using your strengths.

Score = 65–44
Well done, you should be pleased with the results. You should as a rule have answered most questions as 'routinely' or 'sometimes'. Reflect on the reasons that you put a 'sometimes' response. Write down specific incidents that remind you of times when you did not control your behaviour or display the characteristics that you would ideally wish to demonstrate. Think about the environment you were in and write down what negative influences were acting on you. Think about what stimulated a chain of emotions and unhelpful responses in you.

Think back to incidents as a child that may be leading you in the present day to assign incorrect motives to the behaviour of others. Think about questions that you could ask others in the future to check out what their motive is for their behaviour or their responses to you. In the future, try to stop yourself proactively from repeating mistakes. Alternatively, catch yourself in the middle and calm yourself or ask for co-operation in others to avoid a poor outcome. Getting a better result will outweigh any temporary feelings of 'losing face' or 'giving ground'

Score = 43–22
The way you act or the responses that you get from others may puzzle you. You may feel misunderstood a significant amount of the time and not understand what you do which gets you the results that frequently occur. Enlist the help of a friend. Learn to ask for specific feedback from others.

Get into a pattern of preparing for, conducting and reflecting on interactions with people. For example, you may have regular meetings both at work, socially or in the community. If you are experiencing regular or ad-hoc difficulties then do some head clearing before the next event. Get a friend to complete the questionnaire as if they are scoring it about you. Go through the responses and discuss with them what happens to you by reflecting on specific events that you have shared or that have been reported by others.

Score = 21–0
Thank you for being so honest. Showing integrity is a great EI strength. You would benefit from doing the exercise in the grades above and doing a course which would help you to increase both your self-awareness and self-regulation. This score does not mean that you necessarily have poor

social skills in relating to others, just that you are not particularly aware of how or why you behave the way you do.

Summary

So far, you have been given information about the number of leading EI assessments for you to consider doing one as part of your development and maturity. You have been told real life stories by individuals who experienced EI development for the first time and by practitioners in the field. You have been given part of my story for the last three to four years using EI assessments and developments for my company's benefit as well as my own. Now you need to make some decisions, even if it is just to reflect on the content of the book for a while.

As you read through the book you were asked to make notes as they occurred to you and to ask yourself:

- Do I want to know what my EQ is at present? Yes or no?
- Does one of the different approaches to EI assessment appeal to me? Does one of the approaches align with my company's competency framework or HRM initiatives?
- Do I want to develop my EI and gain more emotional knowledge, emotional competence and abilities?
- What is my personal Business Case for investment in EI discovery and development?
- What situations in my life could be alleviated by managing them in a more Emotionally Intelligent way?

Development planning

Remember, there are two types of learning, so cramming or swotting up in books will not enhance your EI significantly.

1 **Cognitive:** Cognitive learning is about absorbing new data and insights into existing frameworks of association and understanding. Emotional learning involves that and more. We also need to engage that part of the brain where our emotional signature is stored. Changing habits such as learning to approach people positively rather than avoiding them, to listen better or to give feedback skilfully is much more challenging than simply adding new data to old.

2 **Emotional:** Emotional learning involves new ways of thinking and acting that are more in tune with our identity – our values and beliefs and attitudes. If you are told to learn a new Word Processing program, you will probably get on with it; however, if you are told that you need to improve control of your temper, you are likely to be upset or offended. Thus the prospect of needing to develop greater emotional intelligence is likely to generate resistance to change. You should test your readiness to change by committing to continue the development started whilst reading this book within 24 hours of closing it.

If you have completed the quiz in this book, you have begun to understand some EI development priorities. Whilst this is an important part of the process, you may find that historical commitments overwhelm you if you go straight to EI development priorities. PDPs are compiled frequently in a well-meaning way. However, real life intervenes: work deadlines and family priorities. The PDP becomes a subject of guilt rather than renewal. Generating fewer, more realistic learning outcomes with sensible milestones should achieve better results and high morale.

Decide what life/work balance is important to you, discuss it with people close to you and come up with a workable scheme to generate some space in your life for you. This may entail renegotiations of existing relationships with partners and children, co-workers, bosses, friends and family.

Consider asking someone to coach you or set up mutual coaching sessions. If a mentoring scheme is available at work or through a relevant institute, ask to be considered. Prepare a set of desired learning outcomes as part of your preparation.

Review development priorities for changes every month. Have you or the business moved on or become divergent? List what is both urgent and a priority first, then list everything else in order of importance.

Reflection exercises

Our emotional intelligence is both innate and shaped by circumstance and environment. The good news is that it can be enhanced in adulthood. Complete this exercise after a short period of developing an EI competence. Ask the following questions in self-study or with a friend or colleague:

- What was the single most challenging thing about the past two weeks regarding your behaviour change?
- What was the easiest thing about the past two weeks regarding your behaviour change?
- What did you notice about letting go of old behaviours? Did you want to chuck it in and go back to your old ways?
- Did you listen to your internal observer when you didn't feel like sticking to it? What did it say?
- In which situations did you give your power away and not accomplish your goals?
- What do you need to do to continue your successes through the rest of your life? Are there any changes you want to make? Adjust your statement of commitment as necessary.
- What else comes up for you?
- What is related? Use your learning from one area to carry over to another.

Paired exercise

For those concerned with the Emotional Intelligence in their organisation, ask a colleague or friend to work through the following questions with you.

- What are the qualities that you identify as being important to you in the process of leading a change programme?
- What kind of challenges would you need to face to be the kind of leader that you want to be?

- Is there a development gap in the leaders of your organisation in the process of change?
- What do you need to bridge this gap?

Regardless of whether you develop your EI for personal or professional reasons, I firmly believe that doing so can lead you to a happier and healthier life. It certainly has been so far my own journey through the Genesis programme with my team from Consultation Limited. I have also found more enduring and mutually beneficial relationships with my clients. Whatever your motive, enjoy the journey.

Further *Test Your ...* titles from Hodder & Stoughton and the Institute of Management, all at £6.99

0 340 78006 1	Test Your Personality	❏
0 340 78050 9	Test Your Management Style	❏
0 340 78169 6	Test Your Management Skills	❏
0 340 78208 0	Test Your Leadership Skills	❏
0 340 78287 0	Test Your Financial Awareness	❏
0 340 78289 7	Test Your Numeracy	❏
0 340 78288 9	Test Your Literacy	❏
0 340 78290 0	Test Your Potential	❏
0 340 80242 1	Test Your Business Skills	❏
0 340 80243 X	Test Your E-Skills	❏
0 340 80241 3	Test Your Emotional Intelligence	❏
0 340 80240 5	Test Your Personal Skills	❏
0 340 80239 1	Test Your Stress Resilience	❏

All Hodder & Stoughton books are available from your local bookshop or can be ordered direct from the publisher. Just tick the titles you want and fill in the form below. Prices and availability subject to change without notice.

To: Hodder & Stoughton Ltd, Cash Sales Department, Bookpoint, 78 Milton Park, Abingdon, Oxon OX14 4TD. If you have a credit card you may order by
telephone – 01235 400414
      fax – 01235 400454
E-mail address: orders@bookpoint.co.uk

Please enclose a cheque or postal order made payable to Bookpoint Ltd to the value of the cover price and allow the following for postage and packaging:

UK & BFPO: £4.30 for one book; £6.30 for two books; £8.30 for three books.

OVERSEAS & EIRE: £4.80 for one book; £7.10 for 2 or 3 books (surface mail).

Name:

Address: ....

....

....

If you would prefer to pay by credit card, please complete:

Please debit my Visa/Mastercard/Diner's Card/American Express (delete as appropriate) card no:

❏❏❏❏❏❏❏❏❏❏❏❏❏❏❏❏❏❏

Signature .... Expiry date ....